How To Be Happy:
3 Keys to a Joyful Life

Förlag: BoD · Books on Demand, Stockholm, Sverige

Tryck: Libri Plureos GmbH, Hamburg, Tyskland

How To Be Happy: 3 Keys to a Joyful Life

First Edition

Montana Publishing and Media

Author: Jonathan Eriksson

Cover design by: Jonathan Eriksson & Anna Kukleva

ISBN: 978-91-8080-144-7

This book is dedicated to

someone who gave me hope when I needed it the most -

my dear friend

SOFIA TIGER

Contents

Why I Created This Book

So, I dove into every book I could find on happiness, willing to try anything that promised relief. And to my surprise, it worked!

I found myself in a dark place: my girlfriend had just walked away, I had lost touch with nearly all my friends, and I was struggling with my weight. My days blurred together, filled with endless hours of video games and mindless YouTube scrolling. I felt utterly lost, like I was stuck in a pit with no way out. At my lowest, thoughts of ending it all haunted me. Ironically, this wasn't the first time I felt this way. Even when I seemingly had it all—a stunning girlfriend, a lively circle of friends for nights out, gaming sessions, and a loving family—I was still deeply unhappy.

I couldn't comprehend how I could feel so miserable with everything I thought I wanted right at my fingertips.

As I hit rock bottom, a flicker of determination sparked within me: I could either surrender to despair or take a leap into the unknown and see what might change. So, I dove into every book I could find on happiness, willing to try anything that promised relief. And to my surprise, it worked!
There was no grand "Eureka!" moment; rather, it was a gradual ascent, a series of small victories that ignited my hope. I could feel the shifts within me, and each improvement fueled my resolve, guiding me toward a genuine sense of happiness. Now, even as I navigate life's inevitable ups and downs, I've acquired the tools to manage whatever comes my way.

I've devoured countless books on the subject, absorbing wisdom from every corner of the happiness landscape. But I realized that such a journey takes time—time I wished I could have saved. That's why I created this book. Here, you'll find a concise roadmap to happiness, distilled from my experiences and learnings. Let's embark on this journey together and unlock the keys to a more fulfilling life.

Happiness Decoded: Understanding Its Nature and How to Get It

At its core, happiness is linked to certain chemicals in our bodies.

Happiness is a personal experience that differs for everyone. It's not just about enjoying fleeting moments of joy; it's about finding deeper meaning and satisfaction in life. At its core, happiness is linked to certain chemicals in our bodies. While some people might try to chase happiness through drugs for a quick high, there are better, natural ways to boost these "Substances of Happiness" without the negative side effects. Here are the key substances that influence how we feel:

- *Dopamine:* This is the chemical that motivates us to seek rewards.
- *Oxytocin:* Known as the "bonding hormone," it helps us feel connected to others.
- *Serotonin:* This stabilizes our mood and promotes a sense of well-being.
- *Endorphins:* These are natural pain relievers that also lift our spirits.
- *Cortisol*: Often called the stress hormone, managing it is vital for happiness.
- *Testosterone:* While commonly associated with masculinity, it plays a role in overall happiness too.

There are effective ways to influence the creation of these substances, which can significantly impact our feelings of happiness. This book contains 3 keys that nurtures genuine happiness. These "keys to happiness" are:

Key 1: *Good Relationships and Being Likable*
Building positive relationships is one of the most fundamental sources of happiness. By developing your social skills, becoming more empathetic, and learning to build trust with others, you can increase your happiness.

Key 2: *The Power of Gratitude*

The world will be exactly as you perceive it. By focusing on what we're grateful for, we can shift our outlook and trigger the release of happiness-related chemicals in our bodies.

Key 3: *Habits for Happiness*

The choices we make every day affect our happiness. Eating well, staying active, and using our time wisely can help our bodies produce the chemicals that make us feel good.
In the upcoming chapters, We will explore these keys in more detail. These three keys have made a huge difference in my life, and I hope they can positively impact yours as well. Let's start this journey together to discover the keys to lasting happiness!

Key 1: Good Relationships and Being Likable

And as a bonus, by being likable, we also get—greater influence, enhanced persuasiveness, a more thriving love life, and career advancements that can propel you forward. Who wouldn't want to unlock such treasures?

The Impact of Good Relationships on Key Chemicals for Happiness

Healthy relationships are not just a source of emotional support; they also play a crucial role in the biochemical processes that contribute to our overall happiness. Here's how strong social connections influence dopamine, oxytocin, serotonin, endorphins, cortisol, and testosterone, leading to a more joyful and fulfilling life.

Dopamine: *The Pleasure Chemical*

How Relationships Contribute: Positive interactions with friends and loved ones stimulate the release of dopamine, the neurotransmitter associated with pleasure and reward. When you engage in enjoyable activities—like sharing a meal, laughing, or exploring new interests—your brain responds by releasing dopamine.

Path to Happiness: This release not only elevates your mood in the moment but also reinforces the desire to seek out more social experiences. The resulting positive feedback loop encourages you to build and maintain relationships, which further enhances your overall sense of happiness.

Oxytocin: *The Bonding Hormone*

How Relationships Contribute: Often referred to as the "love hormone," oxytocin is released during moments of bonding, such as hugging, cuddling, or simply spending quality time together. This hormone fosters feelings of trust and emotional intimacy.

Path to Happiness: The increased oxytocin levels create a sense of connection and security, which is essential for emotional well-being. As these bonds deepen, so does your sense of belonging, significantly contributing to your happiness.

Serotonin: *The Mood Regulator*

How Relationships Contribute: Healthy social networks positively influence serotonin levels, which play a vital role in regulating mood. Supportive relationships help alleviate feelings of loneliness and depression.

Path to Happiness: Higher serotonin levels promote a more stable and positive emotional state. By surrounding yourself with supportive friends and family, you cultivate an environment that fosters happiness and emotional resilience.

Endorphins: *The Natural Mood Boosters*

How Relationships Contribute: Engaging in fun activities with others, whether it's exercising, playing games, or simply sharing a good laugh, leads to the release of endorphins. These are your body's natural painkillers and mood enhancers.

Path to Happiness: The elevated endorphin levels foster a profound sense of joy and well-being. Shared experiences filled with laughter not only create memorable moments but also reinforce your social bonds, contributing to a happier life.

Cortisol: The Stress Hormone

How Relationships Contribute: Positive relationships act as a buffer against cortisol, the hormone associated with stress. Support from friends and family can help lower cortisol levels, reducing the body's stress response.

Path to Happiness: Lower cortisol levels lead to reduced anxiety and stress, promoting relaxation and a sense of calm. This improvement in mental health enhances your ability to enjoy life and navigate challenges more effectively.

Testosterone: *The Social Enhancer*

How Relationships Contribute: While often linked to physical traits, testosterone also influences social behavior. Healthy relationships can help maintain balanced testosterone levels, enhancing assertiveness and confidence.

Path to Happiness: With improved confidence and social interaction, you become more engaged in your relationships and activities, leading to a more fulfilling and happy life. Moreover, supportive relationships reduce stress, allowing testosterone to thrive.

Conclusion: In summary, good relationships have a profound impact on our emotional and biochemical health. By positively influencing dopamine, oxytocin, serotonin, endorphins, cortisol, and testosterone, these connections lay the groundwork for a happier, more fulfilling life. Investing in your relationships not only enriches your emotional landscape but also sets the stage for lasting happiness and well-being. Embrace the power of connection and watch how it transforms your life!

How to Achieve Good Relationships and Being Likable

As we've seen, one key to a happier life lies in nurturing good relationships. But here's the kicker: becoming more likable is the gateway to those fulfilling connections. And as a bonus, by being likable, we also get—greater influence, enhanced persuasiveness, a more thriving love life, and career advancements that can propel you forward. Who wouldn't want to unlock such treasures?

So, how do you elevate your likability? This book delves into four principles that can dramatically enhance your appeal:

1. Don't Judge and You Won't Be Judged

2. Smile and Act as If People Like You

3. Make People Meaningful and Center the Conversation on Them

4. Be Yourself

Ready to embark on this journey to likability and all the rewards it brings? Let's dive in!

1. DON'T JUDGE AND YOU WON'T BE JUDGED

To kick off this section of the book, let's explore some thought-provoking quotes from various voices on the topic of judgment. These insights will hopefully offer a fresh perspective on how we perceive others and ourselves, setting the stage for a deeper understanding of our journey toward greater likability.

✳✳✳

"Don't criticize them; they are just what

we would be under similar circumstances."

Abraham Lincoln

"...but let us judge not that we be not judged."

Abraham Lincoln

"I am learning to understand

rather than immediately judge."

Bruce Lee

"Be curious, not judgmental."

Walt Whitman

✳✳✳

Keep in mind that when we interact with others, we're not engaging with mere logical beings. Humans are fueled by emotions, biases, pride, and vanity. By setting aside judgment, we create a space where the best in people can flourish, allowing their true selves to shine through.

We naturally gravitate toward those who don't judge for several compelling reasons:

Safety and Comfort: Non-judgmental individuals create a safe space where we can express ourselves without fear of criticism. This fosters a sense of comfort, allowing us to be vulnerable and authentic.

Acceptance and Validation: When someone accepts us as we are, it validates our feelings and experiences. This acceptance builds trust and encourages deeper connections.

Empathy and Understanding: Non-judgmental people often exhibit empathy, demonstrating a genuine interest in understanding our perspectives. This quality makes interactions feel meaningful and supportive.

Reduced Anxiety: Interacting with someone who refrains from judgment alleviates social anxiety, allowing us to relax and engage more freely in conversations.

Encouragement of Growth: Without the weight of judgment, we feel empowered to explore new ideas, share our thoughts, and even admit our mistakes. This nurturing environment promotes personal growth and fosters stronger relationships.

In essence, the absence of judgment creates an atmosphere of trust, acceptance, and encouragement, making us feel valued and understood.

The Pygmalion Effect: The Power of Belief as a Self-Fulfilling Prophecy

Setting the Scene: Imagine a bustling elementary school in California, where the seeds of potential are planted each day. In the 1960s, psychologist Robert Rosenthal embarked on a groundbreaking journey to uncover a fascinating truth: that our expectations can shape reality, particularly in the classroom.

The Experiment: Rosenthal devised a clever experiment to illustrate this phenomenon. He began by administering an IQ test to a classroom full of eager students. Once the results were in, he selected about 20% of them at random, labeling them as "intellectual bloomers." He shared this information with their teacher, Mrs. Johnson, claiming these students were destined for remarkable academic growth.

What Happened:

- *Shifting Teacher Expectations:* Armed with this newfound belief in her students' potential, Mrs. Johnson interacted with the bloomers in transformative ways. Her attention and encouragement flowed generously toward them, fostering an atmosphere ripe for learning. Meanwhile, the rest of the class, unknowingly viewed as less capable, received less of her focus.

- *The Ripple Effect in the Classroom:* As the school year unfolded, the differences in treatment became palpable. The bloomers thrived under Mrs. Johnson's nurturing, igniting their enthusiasm and sparking curiosity. In contrast, the other students missed out on that vital encouragement, their abilities languishing in the shadows.

- *Measuring Transformation:* At the year's end, Rosenthal returned to re-test the students. The results were nothing short of astounding—the so-called bloomers had not only gained significant IQ points but had also blossomed into more confident learners, while their peers showed little improvement.

Unpacking the Findings: This pivotal study revealed a striking truth: the students who were labeled as "intellectual bloomers" flourished because their teacher held high expectations for them. It underscored the remarkable power of belief in fostering student achievement.

Wider Implications: The ramifications of Rosenthal's research extend far beyond one classroom. It serves as a clarion call for educators everywhere to recognize the profound influence their expectations can wield. When teachers believe in their students' potential, they cultivate an environment brimming with possibility, where growth and success become attainable goals for all.

Conclusion - The Transformative Power of Belief: The Pygmalion Effect study is a powerful testament to the idea that expectations shape outcomes. When you choose to understand and believe in the best of others, without judgment, they will rise to meet the greatness you see in them. And who does not want great people around them?

A Surprising Perk: Freedom from Self-Judgment

Here's an intriguing twist: when you stop judging others, you'll find your mind is less harsh on itself. Your perception shapes your reality, and by cultivating a positive mindset and refraining from judgment, you open the door to a brighter, more uplifting world. This naturally leads us to the next captivating section of the book, where we explore positivity and acting as if people genuinely enjoy your company. Get ready to dive into this fascinating journey!

2. *SMILE AND ACT AS IF PEOPLE LIKE YOU*

We're naturally drawn to those who exude positive energy, and one of the simplest yet most effective ways to amplify that energy is through a smile. That is why we are starting off this part of the book with a fascinating study that uncovers the remarkable impact a smile can have on how others view you.

The Power of a Smile: Unpacking the Study on Likability

In the realm of human interactions, one simple gesture has the potential to bridge gaps and foster connections: the smile. Research into the psychology of likability has revealed that smiling plays a crucial role in how we perceive others and how they perceive us.

The Study

One notable study explored the effects of smiling on perceived likability. Researchers presented participants with photographs of individuals who either smiled or had neutral expressions. Participants were then asked to rate these individuals on various traits, including warmth, approachability, and overall likability.

Key Findings

1. *Instant Connection:* The results were striking. Smiling individuals were consistently rated as more likable and approachable compared to their non-smiling counterparts. This immediate reaction suggests that a smile can serve as a powerful social signal, indicating friendliness and openness.

2. *Warmth and Trust:* Beyond mere likability, the study highlighted that smiling is often associated with warmth and trustworthiness. People tend to view those who smile as more sincere and empathetic, fostering a deeper sense of connection.

3. *Influence on Interactions:* The impact of a smile extends beyond initial impressions. Those who smile are not only perceived as more likable but are also more likely to receive positive responses in social interactions. This can create a positive feedback loop, where smiling leads to more engaging conversations and stronger relationships.

4. *Cultural Universality:* Interestingly, the effects of smiling on likability appear to transcend cultural boundaries. Across various cultures, a smile is generally interpreted as a sign of friendliness, enhancing its effectiveness in building connections.

Conclusion: The study on likability and smiling underscores the importance of this simple yet powerful gesture in human interactions. A smile can act as a catalyst for connection, warmth, and trust, making us more approachable and likable. By harnessing the power of a smile, we can create more positive interactions and deepen our relationships with others. So, the next time you enter a room or engage with someone new, remember: a smile might just be your best asset.

Acting as if people already like you

Now that we understand how a smile can enhance your relationships, let's uncover another powerful secret to deepening your connections with others. Acting as if people already like you can significantly enhance your likability in several compelling ways:

Positive Energy: When you project confidence and warmth, it creates a positive atmosphere. People are naturally drawn to those who radiate positivity, and your demeanor can encourage them to respond in kind.

Self-Fulfilling Prophecy: Believing that others appreciate you can lead to more authentic interactions. This self-fulfilling prophecy means that your behavior may prompt others to actually like you more because you're embodying qualities that make you likable—like openness and enthusiasm.

Reduced Anxiety: When you act as if people like you, you lower your own social anxiety. This relaxed attitude allows for more genuine interactions, fostering deeper connections.

People tend to gravitate toward those who seem at ease, making you more approachable.

Increased Engagement: Assuming people have a positive view of you encourages more engagement in conversations. You're likely to ask questions, share experiences, and actively listen, which can deepen connections and enhance likability.

Encouraging Reciprocity: When you treat others as if they already hold a favorable view of you, it often inspires them to reciprocate. This mutual positivity creates a reinforcing cycle of goodwill and connection, further enhancing your likability.

Conclusion: Acting like people already like you not only boosts your own confidence but also creates a welcoming environment for meaningful connections. By embodying positivity and openness, you set the stage for others to respond positively, ultimately leading to greater likability and stronger relationships.

3. MAKE PEOPLE MEANINGFUL AND MAKE IT ABOUT THEM

Making people feel truly meaningful and shifting the focus onto them not only enriches our interactions but also significantly boosts our likability in several compelling and transformative ways that can deepen relationships and foster a sense of community.

Creating a Sense of Value: When you prioritize others in conversations, it conveys that you genuinely value their thoughts and experiences. This acknowledgment fosters a sense of significance, making them feel appreciated and enhancing their perception of you.

Building Trust: Showing interest in someone else's life encourages trust. When people sense that you care about them, they are more likely to open up and engage, leading to deeper, more authentic relationships.

Encouraging Engagement: Focusing on others invites them to share more about themselves. Asking questions and actively listening not only deepens connections but also makes interactions feel more dynamic and rewarding.

Creating Memorable Interactions: People remember how you make them feel. By making them the center of attention and showing genuine interest, you create memorable experiences that leave a lasting impression, solidifying your likability.

So, how can we truly make others feel meaningful and center our interactions around them? The answer lies in two powerful strategies: active listening and heartfelt compliments. But before we dive into these transformative practices, let's ignite our motivation with some thought-provoking quotes that beautifully capture the essence of connection and appreciation.

✳✳✳

"The deepest urge in human nature

is the desire to be important."

John Dewey

"The deepest principle of human nature

is a craving to be appreciated."

William James

"If you tell me how you get your feeling of importance,

I'll tell you what you are."

Dale Carnegie

"Listening is a magnetic and strange thing, a creative force. The friends who listen to us are the ones we move toward. When we are listened to, it creates us, makes us unfold and expand."

Karl A. Menninger

✳✳✳

A Guide to Being a Good Active Listener

Armed with those insightful quotes, we're ready to embark on a journey into the art of active listening. This skill not only honors the other person's presence but also ensures they feel genuinely valued and that the conversation revolves around their unique experiences. Let's uncover the secrets to making every interaction impactful. Here's a step-by-step guide to help you master this art:

Be Present

- Eliminate Distractions: Put away your phone and minimize background noise. Focus entirely on the person speaking.

- Maintain Eye Contact: Show engagement by looking at the speaker, which helps convey your interest.

Use Open Body Language

- Face the Speaker: Position your body towards them to demonstrate your attentiveness.

- Nod and Smile: Use non-verbal cues to show you're following along and encourage them to continue.

Practice Reflective Listening

- Paraphrase: Repeat back what the speaker has said in your own words to show you understand. For example, "So what you're saying is..."

- Ask Clarifying Questions: If something isn't clear, ask questions to gain a better understanding. This shows you're genuinely interested in their perspective.

Validate Their Feelings

- Acknowledge Emotions: Recognize and validate the speaker's feelings. Phrases like, "I can see that this is really important to you," can make a big difference.

- Avoid Dismissing Concerns: Even if you disagree, acknowledge their feelings as valid and important.

Avoid Interrupting

- Let Them Finish: Resist the urge to interject or finish their sentences. Allow them to express their thoughts fully before responding.

- Hold Your Responses: Take a moment to reflect on what they've said before you reply.

Engage with Empathy

- Put Yourself in Their Shoes: Try to understand their perspective and feelings. This creates a deeper connection and shows that you care.

- Share Similar Experiences (if appropriate): Relating your own experiences can enhance connection, but ensure it doesn't shift the focus away from them.

Follow Up

- Summarize Key Points: At the end of the conversation, summarize the main points to reinforce your understanding.

- Check In Later: If the conversation was significant, follow up later to show that you care and remember what was discussed.

Give Compliments and Positive Feedback

- Highlight Their Strengths: Recognize their insights or bravery in sharing. For example, "I really appreciate how open you were about this."

- Encourage Further Discussion: Invite them to share more by asking open-ended questions, like, "What do you think about...?"

The Final Takeaways on Active Listening: By mastering the art of active listening, you not only make others feel important and valued, but you also cultivate deeper, more meaningful connections. Remember, it's about creating a safe space where people feel heard and appreciated. Your attentive presence can make all the difference! As we've touched on earlier, one key element of being an exceptional active listener is the art of giving compliments. Now, let's dive deeper into this transformative practice and explore how thoughtful praise can enrich our interactions and uplift those around us!

The Power of Compliments

Giving compliments can significantly enhance your likability for several compelling reasons:

Boosts Others' Self-Esteem: Compliments make people feel valued and appreciated. When you acknowledge someone's strengths or achievements, it boosts their self-esteem, and they are more likely to enjoy your company.

Creates Positive Energy: Compliments create a warm, positive atmosphere. People are naturally drawn to those who uplift and encourage them, making you more approachable and likable.

Builds Trust and Connection: Offering genuine compliments fosters trust and rapport. It shows that you pay attention to others and recognize their qualities, which helps deepen connections.

Encourages Reciprocity: When you compliment someone, they may feel compelled to return the favor, creating a cycle of positivity. This exchange reinforces social bonds and enhances mutual appreciation.

Demonstrates Empathy: Compliments indicate that you are empathetic and aware of others' feelings. This quality makes you more relatable and likable, as people appreciate those who understand and acknowledge their experiences.

In essence, giving compliments not only enriches your relationships but also positions you as a positive force in others' lives, making you inherently more likable.

A Guide to Giving Meaningful Compliments

Be Genuine

- Authenticity Matters: Always ensure your compliments come from the heart. Sincere praise is more impactful than generic statements.

Choose the Right Moment

- Timing is Key: Deliver compliments at moments when they can have the most impact, such as after someone achieves something significant or when they seem down.

- Private vs. Public: Consider the setting. Some people thrive on public recognition, while others might prefer a private conversation.

Use Positive Body Language

- Eye Contact: Maintain eye contact to show that you genuinely mean what you're saying.

- Warmth in Your Tone: Use a friendly and warm tone to convey sincerity and kindness.

Highlight Personal Qualities

- Acknowledge Character Traits: When giving compliments, it's essential to recognize and celebrate the unique character traits that define a person.

- Celebrate Their Efforts: Recognize hard work: "I can see how much effort you put into this project; it truly shows."

Encourage Their Strengths

- Reinforce Skills: If someone has a talent or skill, acknowledge it: "You have a remarkable ability to connect with people; it's a gift."

- Be Specific: Instead of saying "You're great," try something more detailed, like "I really admire how you organized that project; your attention to detail was impressive." This not only appreciates their work but also encourages them to continue striving for excellence.

Follow Up

- Keep the Conversation Going: After giving a compliment, ask a question related to it: "I loved your presentation! What inspired you to choose that topic?"

- Express Continued Support: Reinforce your compliment by expressing excitement for their future achievements.

Be Mindful of Cultural Differences

- Understand Context: Different cultures may perceive compliments differently. Adjust your approach based on what feels appropriate for the individual.

The Final Takeaways on Giving Meaningful Compliments: By following these steps, you can become skilled at giving compliments that uplift others and foster deeper connections. Remember, a well-timed and sincere compliment can brighten someone's day and strengthen your relationships! Practice these techniques consistently, and watch how your interactions transform.

4. *BE YOURSELF*

The Magnetic Power of Being Yourself

Embracing your true self isn't just a personal journey; it's a powerful magnet for enhancing your likability. Here's why authenticity can transform your connections:

Authenticity Attracts Authenticity: When you dare to show your true colors, you naturally draw in those who appreciate you for exactly who you are. Authenticity creates genuine connections, sparking interest and camaraderie with others who are equally comfortable in their own skin. This mutual appreciation lays the groundwork for relationships that are not just stronger, but deeply meaningful.

Building Trust: Genuineness breeds trust. When others sense your transparency, they feel secure in their interactions with you. Trust is the bedrock of likability; once established, it opens the door for deeper conversations and positive engagements.

Reducing Social Anxiety: Pretending to be someone you're not can lead to crippling anxiety. By embracing your true self, you lift that burden, allowing for a more relaxed and confident presence in social settings. This ease makes you more approachable, making others want to engage with you.

Encouraging Vulnerability: When you reveal your authentic self, you invite others to do the same. Sharing your thoughts, experiences, and even your flaws creates a safe space for vulnerability. This openness fosters deeper bonds, enriching your connections and enhancing your likability. Ultimately, we appreciate people who are human and show vulnerability because it creates genuine connections and fosters a sense of belonging.

Unique Value: Every individual is a treasure trove of unique qualities and perspectives. By being yourself, you highlight these traits, setting yourself apart from the crowd. People are often captivated by originality, and your distinctiveness can ignite admiration and intrigue.

Consistency: Authenticity fosters a consistent persona. When you're true to yourself, you cultivate reliability, making it easier for others to understand and trust you. This stability enhances likability, as people appreciate knowing what to expect.

The Final Takeaways on The Magnetic Power of Being Yourself: Ultimately, being yourself is more than just a likability strategy; it's the foundation for forging genuine connections. By celebrating your individuality, you create a welcoming space for others to engage, connect, and truly appreciate you. Authenticity invites authenticity, and that shared recognition is the secret ingredient to lasting likability.

Key 2: The Power of Gratitude

*Our reality is a reflection of our perceptions—
how we see the world shapes the world we experience.*

The Impact of Gratitude on Key Chemicals for Happiness

Our perceptions are shaped by our focus. When we center our attention on gratitude, we begin to notice the goodness in our lives, transforming our reality into one filled with positivity and joy. Imagine a simple practice that not only uplifts your mood but also reshapes your brain chemistry for the better. Enter gratitude—a powerful force that can significantly enhance your happiness by influencing the very chemicals in your body. Here's a closer look at how gratitude transforms your emotional landscape through key neurotransmitters and hormones:

Dopamine: The Joy Catalyst

Gratitude is like a spark that ignites dopamine, the brain's "feel-good" chemical. When you pause to appreciate the good things in your life, your brain responds with a rush of pleasure and reward. This dopamine boost creates a tantalizing cycle: the more you acknowledge your blessings, the more joy you invite into your life, making gratitude a delightful habit that fuels happiness.

Oxytocin: The Connection Enhancer

When you express gratitude, you're not just acknowledging what's good; you're strengthening your bonds with others. This heartfelt appreciation releases oxytocin, often dubbed the "love hormone," which fosters trust and emotional intimacy. As oxytocin flows, so do feelings of belonging and connection, weaving a rich tapestry of relationships that enhances your overall happiness.

Serotonin: The Mood Stabilizer

Gratitude is a natural elixir for serotonin, a key player in mood regulation. By shifting your focus to the positives, you combat loneliness and despair, elevating your mood to new heights. Elevated serotonin levels promote emotional resilience, enabling you to navigate life's challenges with a brighter outlook and a more stable emotional core.

Endorphins: The Happiness Boosters

Imagine laughter and joy bubbling up from within—this is the magic of endorphins. Practicing gratitude triggers these natural mood enhancers, making you feel lighter and more content. When you celebrate the good in your life, you unleash a wave of endorphins, turning mundane moments into extraordinary experiences filled with joy and fulfillment.

Cortisol: The Stress Buster

Gratitude acts as a shield against stress by lowering cortisol levels, the hormone linked to anxiety and tension. By consciously focusing on what you appreciate, you cultivate a sanctuary of calm in your mind. This shift reduces stress and promotes a sense of tranquility, paving the way for better mental health and a more relaxed existence.

Testosterone: The Confidence Booster

While often associated with physical attributes, testosterone also plays a vital role in your emotional landscape. Engaging in gratitude can enhance feelings of assertiveness and self-worth. When you appreciate yourself and your surroundings, you naturally boost your confidence, empowering you to engage more fully with the world.

Conclusion: In essence, practicing gratitude is a simple yet profound way to enhance happiness through a complex interplay of neurotransmitters and hormones. By fostering positive emotions, deepening social connections, and reducing stress, gratitude serves as a powerful tool for improving overall well-being. Embracing gratitude not only enriches our lives but also transforms the very chemistry of our bodies, paving the way for a happier, more fulfilling existence.

How to Integrate Gratitude into your Daily Life

Our reality is a reflection of our perceptions— how we see the world shapes the world we experience. So why not actively shape our reality each day to make it extraordinary? Embracing gratitude as a means to cultivate happiness can be a truly transformative practice. Here are some powerful ways to weave gratitude into your daily life:

Keep a Gratitude Journal

- Daily Entries: Dedicate a few minutes each day to jot down three to five things you're grateful for. These can be small moments, like a warm cup of coffee or a kind word from a friend.

- Reflect on Positive Experiences: Take time to reflect on the positive experiences of the day, no matter how minor they seem.

Express Gratitude to Others

- Send Thank-You Notes: Write heartfelt notes or messages to people who have impacted your life, acknowledging their contributions and how they've made you feel.

- Verbal Acknowledgment: Make it a habit to verbally express appreciation. Compliment a colleague, thank a friend for their support, or acknowledge your family members for their efforts.

Practice Mindfulness

- Gratitude Meditation: Incorporate gratitude into your meditation practice by focusing on what you appreciate in your life. Visualize those moments and feel the associated emotions.

- Mindful Moments: Throughout the day, pause to notice and appreciate the beauty around you—nature, relationships, or simple joys.

Create Gratitude Rituals

- Morning or Evening Rituals: Start or end your day by reflecting on what you're thankful for. This can set a positive tone for your day or provide closure at night.

- Family Gratitude Practices: Encourage family discussions about gratitude during meals or special occasions, fostering a collective appreciation.

Shift Your Perspective

- Reframe Challenges: When faced with difficulties, try to identify lessons or positive aspects. This shift in perspective can help you see challenges as opportunities for growth.

- Focus on the Present: Remind yourself to appreciate the present moment instead of constantly looking to the future for happiness.

Engage in Acts of Kindness

- Random Acts of Kindness: Performing small acts of kindness can amplify your sense of gratitude. Helping others often leads to feelings of joy and fulfillment.

- Volunteer: Engaging in community service can enhance your gratitude by providing perspective on your own circumstances and fostering a sense of connection.

Cultivate Gratitude in Relationships

- Appreciate Loved Ones: Regularly acknowledge and express gratitude for the people in your life. This can strengthen your bonds and deepen your relationships.

- Create Gratitude Circles: Initiate conversations with friends or family where everyone shares what they're grateful for, fostering a positive and uplifting atmosphere.

The Final Takeaways on How to integrate gratitude into your daily life: By intentionally weaving gratitude into your daily routine, you create a powerful antidote to negativity and stress. This practice not only enhances your mood but also fosters a deeper connection with yourself and others, paving the way for a happier, more fulfilled life.

Key 3: Habits for Happiness

With this understanding, we have the tools to live a more Joyful Life!

Categorizing Our Happiness Habits into Three Areas

Every day, we navigate a sea of habits, some rooted in our conscious choices and others hidden in the shadows of our routines. Imagine the transformative power of recognizing these habits and intentionally choosing those that elevate your happiness!

As we've uncovered, six vital chemicals—dopamine, oxytocin, serotonin, endorphins, cortisol, and testosterone—play a pivotal role in shaping our emotional landscape. Among these, dopamine emerges as a key player, influencing every facet of our lives. When wielded wisely, it can elevate our experiences; when mismanaged, it creates ripples that can disrupt our overall well-being and influence all the other vital chemicals.

To guide you on this journey toward joy, I've categorized our happiness habits into three distinct categories: **Mental Habits**, **Physical Habits**, and because of its tremendous impact on our well being and all the other chemicals, **Dopamine Habits**. Each category offers insights into how you can consciously cultivate a more fulfilling life, where every choice contributes to your happiness!

Mental Habits

True happiness emerges from the search for meaning in our lives. We're not designed to feel joyful all the time; life can be tough and unpredictable. Yet, when you have a purpose, even the hardest moments become temporary. Just as the sun rises and sets, both joy and sorrow will inevitably pass. Embrace the journey, for every moment—good or bad—shapes your story and propels you forward.

We've already explored the power of gratitude and the importance of not judging others—two essential mental habits that nurture happiness. But there are more strategies you can adopt to cultivate joy. This book delves into two transformative habits that can truly change the game: "The Power of Choice: Transforming Stress into Joy" and **"Embracing Positivity"**. Prepare to unlock the potential within you and discover how these practices can elevate your life!

The Power of Choice: Transforming Stress into Joy
One intriguing mental habit influences how your body manages cortisol, the stress hormone that impacts your sense of well-being. Take exercise as an example. While it releases feel-good chemicals, if you approach it with a mindset of obligation—"I have to do this"—you might also trigger stress responses. The secret lies in your motivation: find joy in the movement itself.

Think about it: when you exercise, you're making a choice. You might want to get fit, and that's a great goal! Embrace the chance to be active and appreciate what your body can do. Focus on the positive motivations behind your actions, whether you're working, socializing, or facing a daunting task. Ask yourself: why do I go to work? Sure, there's the paycheck, but it's also about providing for yourself and creating memorable experiences.

Change your mindset, and watch remarkable things unfold!

Embracing Positivity

Embracing positivity transformed my life in ways I never imagined. Deep down, I always knew that staying positive was essential, but it wasn't until I fully committed to this mindset that I discovered its true power. Remember: Our reality is a reflection of our perceptions— how we see the world shapes the world we experience.

I made a conscious choice to focus only on the positive aspects of my life, refusing to harbor even a single negative thought about others. And just like that—*poof!*—everything changed. I used to struggle to connect with people, often fixating on their flaws. But as I trained my mind to see the good in others, they blossomed before my eyes—becoming more engaging, intelligent, and kind. It was a revelation that ignited my spirit!

This newfound positivity didn't just change how I viewed others; it transformed how I saw myself. My meals tasted more delicious, my sheets felt cozier, and my entire life radiated with brightness. Embracing positivity is one of the greatest habits you can cultivate for happiness. When you shift your focus from what's wrong to what's right, you'll watch the negatives fade away.

So take that step! Choose to see the good in yourself and in the world around you. As you do, you'll uncover a life filled with joy and endless possibilities!

Physical Habits

Our minds and the release of those happiness-boosting chemicals we've explored are deeply intertwined with our bodies. The impact of our physical habits on our emotional well-being is truly remarkable. In this section, we'll dive into two vital factors that can elevate your happiness: **Exercise** and **Nutrition**. Embrace these powerful tools, and watch as they transform not just your body, but your entire outlook on life! You have the power to boost your mood and enhance your well-being—let's unlock that potential together!

Exercise

Our bodies are designed for movement, and when we embrace exercise, we ignite the release of the happiness chemicals that uplift our spirits. Let's explore how different types of exercise stimulate the production of dopamine, oxytocin, serotonin, endorphins, cortisol, and testosterone:

Dopamine

- Release Mechanism: Exercise stimulates the brain's reward system, promoting the release of dopamine, which enhances feelings of pleasure and motivation.
- Impact: Regular physical activity can help improve mood, increase motivation, and combat feelings of anxiety and depression.

Oxytocin

- Release Mechanism: While not exclusively linked to exercise, physical activity, especially in a social setting (like group classes or team sports), can boost oxytocin levels.
Impact: This hormone fosters feelings of connection and trust, enhancing social bonds and overall emotional well-being.

Serotonin

- Release Mechanism: Exercise increases the availability of tryptophan, the precursor to serotonin. Aerobic activities, in particular, can enhance serotonin production.
- Impact: Elevated serotonin levels contribute to improved mood, reduced anxiety, and enhanced feelings of well-being.

Endorphins

- Release Mechanism: Physical activity, especially vigorous exercise, triggers the release of endorphins—chemicals that act as natural painkillers.
- Impact: Often referred to as the "runner's high," endorphins create feelings of euphoria, reduce stress, and improve mood, making exercise a powerful antidote to anxiety and depression.

Cortisol
- Release Mechanism: Exercise can temporarily elevate cortisol levels, especially during intense workouts. However, regular, moderate exercise helps regulate and lower baseline cortisol levels over time.
- Impact: Managing cortisol through consistent physical activity can help reduce stress and anxiety, leading to better overall mental health.

Testosterone
- Release Mechanism: Resistance training and high-intensity interval training (HIIT) can stimulate testosterone production.
- Impact: Increased testosterone levels contribute to improved mood, higher energy levels, and enhanced motivation, as well as muscle growth and physical strength.

Conclusion: Incorporating regular exercise into your routine can significantly influence the release of these hormones and neurotransmitters, promoting improved mood, increased energy, and overall well-being. Whether through aerobic activities, strength training, or even social workouts, the benefits of exercise extend far beyond the physical, enhancing your mental and emotional health as well.

Nutrition

I used to struggle with relentless low energy, stress, and mood swings, feeling sluggish and irritable—and I was constantly hungry! One day, I decided to experiment: what if I only ate the foods that are hailed as the best for the body? The transformation was astonishing. My energy surged, my mood stabilized, and my sleep improved. It became crystal clear: our minds and bodies are deeply interconnected, and what we consume matters immensely. If you're seeking greater happiness, it's essential to explore how food impacts your well-being. Your plate could be the key to a brighter, more vibrant life!

Dopamine Habits

Last but certainly not least, this book will culminate in a revelation that transformed my entire perspective on life: the profound impact of dopamine on our human experience. I'll kick things off with two thought experiments that reshaped how I view joy and fulfillment.

Consider this: when we talk about enjoying life, let's break it down. Picture this: if I indulge in a chocolate bar, I'll experience a brief sugar rush—about 15 minutes of bliss—followed by a sluggish dip that lingers for hours. Now, if I opt for a nutritious meal packed with energy-boosting goodness, the initial satisfaction might not match that quick high, but the benefits will resonate far longer, leaving me feeling revitalized and energized. And let's not forget the long-term effects of cultivating such habits!

Now, imagine this scenario:
Scenario 1: You're in your kitchen, munching on a burger. It's decent—satisfying, but nothing to write home about.
Scenario 2: You find yourself on a deserted island, having gone a week without food. When you finally get that same burger, it tastes like pure ecstasy.

This illustrates a powerful truth: our experiences are shaped not just by the things themselves, but by our relationship with them. The way we perceive joy can be redefined, revealing deeper layers of fulfillment. Join me as we dive into the world of dopamine and discover how it can elevate our lives!

Understanding Dopamine and How to Harness It for Happiness

Dopamine is a neurotransmitter that plays a crucial role in the brain's reward system, influencing our feelings of pleasure and motivation. It regulates mood, cognitive functions, and motor control, making it essential for everyday life. When dopamine levels are imbalanced, it can lead to mood disorders, addiction, and issues with movement.

Let's look at an example of how dopamine operates: When you watch content on your phone, like YouTube videos, your brain releases dopamine. This creates a craving for more, prompting you to scroll endlessly. However, over time, your brain becomes desensitized, causing the dopamine highs to fade. As a result, activities like engaging in conversation can feel dull or unsatisfying because your dopamine levels are depleted. The same phenomenon occurs with food; indulging in candy provides an initial rush, but soon you find yourself seeking more to achieve that same high. This pattern resembles the effects seen with drugs, even if the consequences differ. So, should we avoid all pleasurable activities? Absolutely not! Dopamine is a driving force that propels us forward and brings joy.

I categorize dopamine-driven habits into two types: *Active Dopamine* and *Passive Dopamine.*

Active Dopamine comes from engaging in activities that stimulate your body and mind—like exercising, socializing, writing, or singing. After these activities, you typically feel a sense of uplift and satisfaction.

Passive Dopamine, on the other hand, results from inactivity and can leave you feeling drained. Activities like binge-watching videos, mindlessly scrolling, or overeating often lead to a dip in mood rather than an uplift. Essentially, passive dopamine comes from experiences where you're inactive.

Remember: Our experiences are shaped not just by the activities themselves, but by our relationship with them. By minimizing passive dopamine, we can enhance the enjoyment of active dopamine pursuits. This insight allows us to be mindful of how our bodies respond to dopamine, empowering us to shape our lives and cultivate happiness. With this understanding, we have the tools to live a more Joyful Life!

The Journey Continues

"A journey of a thousand miles begins with a single step."
Lao Tzu

I want to take a moment to express my heartfelt gratitude for your choice to dive into this book. From the very beginning, my goal has been to share the transformative insights that have guided me on my journey toward greater happiness. If this book has helped you in any way, it fills my heart with immense joy!

Life is an extraordinary adventure, filled with twists, turns, and challenges that can test our resolve. While I am fortunate to experience a life rich with joy, I also encounter inevitable bumps along the way—moments that push me to grow and adapt. These challenges are not obstacles; they are stepping stones that teach us invaluable lessons and help us become who we are meant to be.

The keys outlined in this book are not mere concepts; they are powerful tools I actively integrate into my daily life. This journey requires commitment, resilience, and a willingness to embrace both the highs and lows as essential parts of the process.

If you feel inspired to adopt these keys for yourself, remember: this journey is uniquely yours. It's not just about reaching a destination; it's about the growth, discovery, and transformation that happen along the way. Every step you take, every lesson learned, adds richness and meaning to your life.
Embrace this journey with open arms and a courageous heart. Celebrate your victories, no matter how small, and view challenges as opportunities to learn and evolve. Every moment is a chance for joy, connection, and self-discovery. So step boldly into your life, knowing that you have the power to create your own happiness and shape your future. The adventure is yours—let it unfold and embrace every moment!

About The Author

Jonathan Eriksson

A multifaceted Swedish writer, philosopher, poet, and artist, dedicated to moving audiences and inspiring individuals through his diverse expressions. In his own words, he says, "In everything I do, my aspiration is to be a positive force in people's lives. I strive to contribute to their unlocking of their best selves." With a robust academic foundation, Jonathan has spent six years studying the intricacies of the human mind and its profound influences. His insights blend scholarly knowledge with artistic creativity, offering a unique perspective on personal growth. Jonathan resides in his cherished hometown of Umeå, celebrated for its stunning natural landscapes, where he enjoys life with his family amidst the beauty that fuels his inspiration.